CONFETTI DUSTS

THE FREE FLOWING LINGERS

Thelioness.onpaper

BookLeaf Publishing

India | USA | UK

Presentation by *BookLeaf Publishing*

Web: www.bookleafpub.com

E-mail: info@bookleafpub.com

ISBN: 9789358739107

First edition 2021

ACKNOWLEDGEMENT

I would like to thank God for all the blessings , all the beautiful people and all the experiences that shaped my journey. Gifting me the courage , love and the ability to get through days and nights with strength to keep going.

Surrounding me with all his beautiful creations, the very gravels to sparkly inspirations and showing me how fortunate I am to be alive everyday.

I would like to thank my mother for showing how a woman can be a mother, a wife, a business owner and an athlete all in the same time. love you so much mom. You are a beautiful human being.

I would like to thank my father for teaching how to truly remove negativity and unwanted energy out of my life. Showing me how to hold my shields up high. Thank you dad. Much love. You are a true inspiration.

I would like to thank my loving sister for her support throughout my journey in life in every decision I have taken. And thank you for supporting me throughout the making of my book too. Love you and thank you for everything

I would like to give my gratitude to my beautiful twin cousins. My pillars ! You both are such extraordinary individuals. Thank you for guiding me through my journeys in life. For showing me that there is beauty in my strength. Introducing me to platforms where I could enhance my craftsmanship . Allowing me to see and believe that with your heart set on, achievements in life can be endlessly beautiful. Constantly shining a light on my darkest moments. Giving me a safe space in your hearts to let my vulnerabilities flow freely. Thank you for encouraging me to write this book and helping me through every process. Thank you for your beautiful son , my awesome brilliant little cousin who not only makes my days much more brighter but also makes me think much more wiser. Thank you for your love. Thank you for inspiring me to be the best version of myself everyday. I love the three of you so very much.

Thank you to the handful of friends who have been around in my life. Catching up and making sure I'm okay.

I would like to thank the abusers I have once loved. Leaving monsters under my bed. They gave me reasons to write.

Thank you to everyone who gave me strengths, weaknesses , tears and laughter.

I would like to thank the pain and the joys , life have to offer over the years of my existence.

And thank you to ones who are currently reading this book.
For taking time to read my thoughts on paper.

Thank you so very much. You are all deeply appreciated.

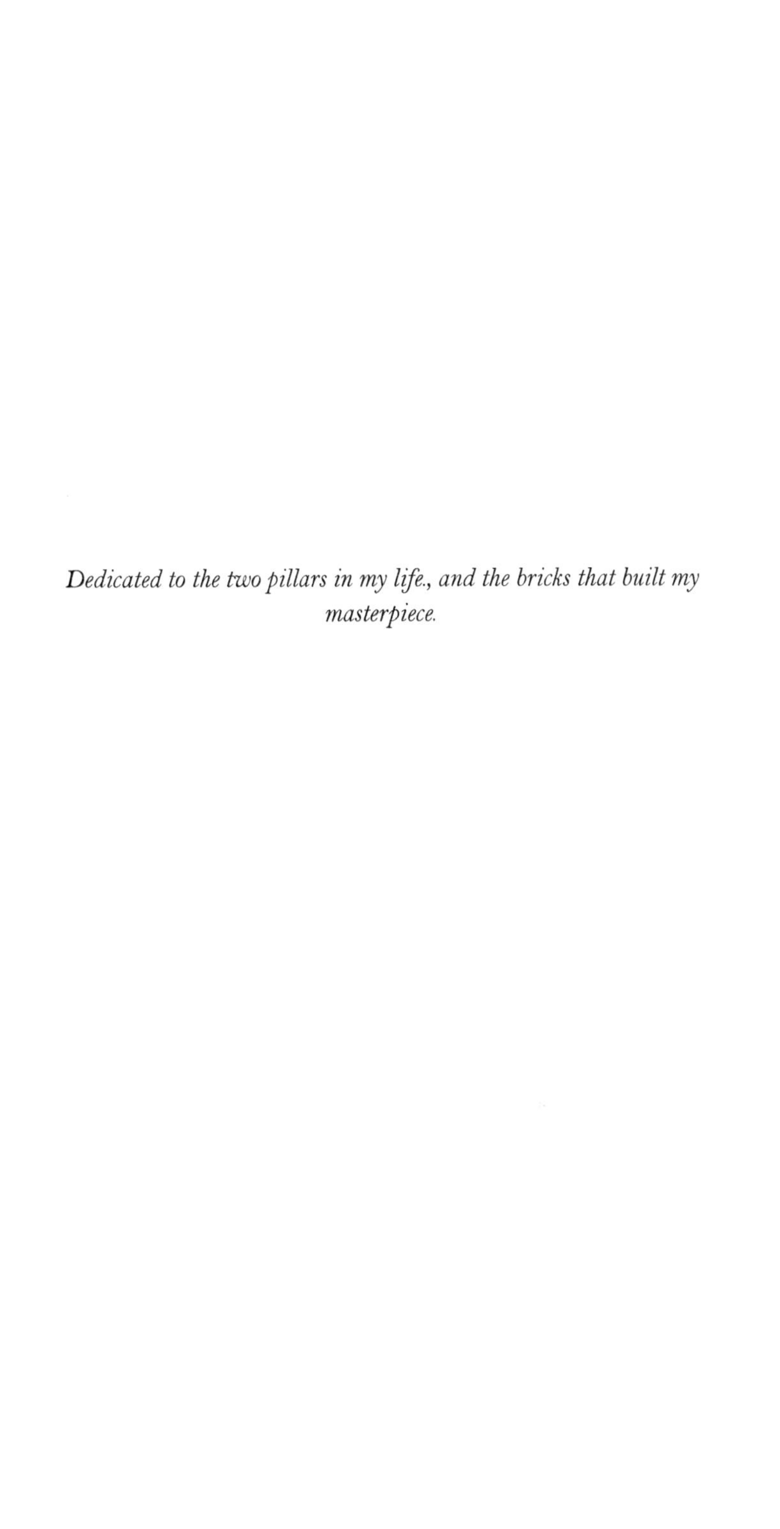

Dedicated to the two pillars in my life., and the bricks that built my masterpiece.

PREFACE

"We are all broken, that's how the light gets in." —Ernest Hemingway

"Laugh loudly, laugh often, and most important, laugh at yourself." — Chelsea Handler

1. PERVERTED PALMS

To the man who spread spell binding words in to the ears of a little girl,

Expecting her to read between the lines of a lust language she hardly understood,

How did her unprovocative gaze permit him to advance in such hunger ? I wonder..

Ignoring the delicate frail tones in her silent tears ,

As he bed his perversive palms on to her hybrid skin,

Breaking into every chambers of her untouched body ,

She would use the darkness to hush her resistance,

Feeling like the targeted still board from the game of darts,

Confused in the abuse that painted her nights ,

She became his consistent mid night ice-cold sandwich,

Her trembling knees would cry so loud that Lucifer would not dare utter a word during his feast,

The flicker in his eyes would tell her that he is no where near done with her,

Her silent hisses would not stand a chance against his cruel needs ,

Being bitten in the back of her innocence, she would question,

What would anyone anymore need from what's thrown into the trash?

Destructive thoughts roamed around her head ,

Like a cyclone of wasps coiling in her mind,

While his ego, so easily build over her grief,

Her pages were left with aggressive punctuation scar marks ,

Shame hiding under the scribbles of her harbouring fears,

As night terrors ate away any piece of flesh left in her ,

Endless falling into what felt like a bottomless pit with no knowledge of if or when the day light shall begin.

2. MISPLACED LOVE

Form of poetry (sonnet)

Quiet evening sky , buttered in gray clouds,

Floating over those Storied gasps of grass,

Kicking sands in the eyes of raging crowds,

When you stand on top of the feet of brass,

Words of you ,a simple love rant rivers,

Such visions you had of taste but covered,

Acting to lust with kisses of shivers,

I see your skin spilled ink from lies hovered,

Tired of filling our lost empty space,

When nowhere in you could desire women,

Needing you to need my broken heart's face,

Under the lights you once thrived to listen,

So selfish to want the love lost in you,

Guess I imagined our flame somehow grew.

3. BEFORE!

There was a time before my tears swamped my room into a lake,

Before my pages became a Scribble of shame

Before my canvas knew the colours of blood charcoal,

Before the stains used to easily fade,

Before the "discipline " beatings felt like mosquito bites,

Before I so badly wanted to tape my eyes shut through those foul nights

Before my inner voice turned out to be my own pistol,

Before demons hijacked my joy, my tranquillity,

Now, till the end before my tomorrow's let this be the most I ever see,

Before tomorrow's maggots embrace my dyeing flesh,

Before tomorrow's sun watches, let this be the most I ever breath,

Before tomorrow see me let my heart be the brightest side of the moon,

Before tomorrow's winter rises, let my bones be the utmost human the seasons ever see.

4. IMAGINE THE CONFUSION

Imagine coming from men who do not understand why they were brought to this earth,

Humour behind my confusion, well, at-least laughs left less room for explanation,

Imagine mistakes coming from your own family rather than the family you chose,

Your cartilage being torn apart to pieces by the lineage that were supposed to hand you down heirlooms,

Landmarked into a defaced and defiled unbecoming creature,

Prohibited to primp the way you primp or eat the way you eat or breath the way you breathe,

"You are nothing like the woman you came from", they say.

And somehow sneaking in reverse-psychology, racially inappropriate sexist opinions,

With the night cold air between you and "locals" you start to feel like an alien in the midst of serpents ,

A centaur among a rangale of stags,

Finding home within the rare needles buried under 500 feet mountain of hay stacks,

Glistening larger than life, more than anyone can ever realize
how woman enough it takes to be you,

Being asked and begged to be chopped into bite sized pieces,

Just so the rest could dine easier on you,

So why go through all that hassle for their convenience
shadowing all your inconvenience,

If they could they might as well swallow you all

As a matter of fact, I dare you to dare them,

Why not just take you as a whole?

5. WINGS

I always tend to live in a dream of a million dreams,

With little of what's left on my flesh,

I can feel nefarious violently carving a split through the void
hidden inside,

As the psychotic megalomaniac that constantly attempts to
clip off my flaps,

He failed to see, I could care so little about gravity,

Go ahead! Take away my ability to fly,

Watch me as I carry my blazing smile melting away every
block of ice he throws at me,

I found the beast in me, synthesizing supernatural clap backs,

Wearing the galaxy like perfectly fitted skin,

So try! Sever my lungs wide open and execute me to a blood
eagle,

Let parts of you fall apart to never come back again,

And you will feel through your veins the aggressive loss of
the stained angel's wings.

6. STRENGTH AND BEAUTY

If my memories could speak, oh they would have such
beautiful stories to tell of you,

They would start by your gifted eyes of a dynamic warrior,
sufficient and observant,

Your masked jittering followed by uncontainable explosions
of laughter's,

Spreading them around through latching on cells,

Tainting a room of frowns multiplying them in two by three
by four, they swell,

Your joy, such sweet melodies of heaven, maybe that is why
for a second, I tend to forget all the blizzards,

Brother you have seen peeks of the world and hints of its
unkindness,

Learning how to hold a shield of fire,

You plant seeds of flares in your boots and run around
melting ice blocks that caves in on you,

Mastering scientific sorcery tricks and leaving little spoof
crumbs right before supper,

Recently, you taught me a new game of swimming, "who could float under and swim the farthest? "

I constantly refuse to back down from a challenge and you always win,

I guess maybe I understand, you love the sea for reasons,

Maybe Underwater is the only place that has one language,

And with your feet hovering above the sand you would sing as if no one is watching, sometimes in your own made up lines,

Your mind yielded into the sharpest blade,

Smeared in the most greatest wisdom one could ever ask for,

You could predict the end of an episode before the crime ever began,

So recognize the beauty of your strengths and the strengths of your beauty,

They hold power within one another, and radiate indestructible blaze through your silhouette.

7. THE MISTRESS THAT BLEEDS INK

Your ink is like a forest fire, bleeding its flame all over the evening azure,

Unstoppable force of nature,

The untameable brilliant sun that glares stronger than any stormy blues,

Come what may, come in shame, Come at her in your back of spines,

And the mistress shall wrap her flaming mane, around your pain of hues.

THE AURA THAT NEVER DRIES OUT OF RHYME.

Heart of a beaming machete full of chimes, slaughtering the clouds of darkness in the light of rhymes,

Spontaneous powerhouse chards of aura,

Allows summer to bloom through a glass of flora,

Next to you the sun would not dare to stand a chance,

In your tones of strength, winter could not share your dance .

8. ALONE

Dialects that exist in too many dictionaries,

Yet I find such strangeness in a sail without a name,

When I have been soaring over the rainbows, misled by my
own misguided words,

How many silly paper butterflies does it take for me to realize
that fake is real?

Much more like the distance between you and I, like the fire
and the sky, like those unforgiving jaws, still stained by the
blood of my broken bones and the deafening silence that
rapidly sinks into a deep dark sin,

I keep screaming at my troubled seas through the tunnels of
my drowning lungs "stop making homes out of men",

Free falling into a rabbit hole with no bottom end,

Grew vengeful claws to undress my soul as I just bite the
pain away,

When darkness are the only eyes that see me,

Terrified to abandon this forbidden dance choreographed in
the chronicles from the devil's tomb,

Why do they say love can love? I still pour my amethyst rain in the haunting pleasure of losing everything,

Rhyming within metaphors never became a part of me but kindly please pardon my pleas,

Within those lilac gaze, shadowy hands were taking back my tears, ripping them out like a malignant tumour,

Yet I will never forget the touch that phased me into complete desertion,

Alone! You, my companion that felt like forever, oh you dunked your so called "you, me, we in us" far too many awful times, just to play a game on a severely broken mind.

9. DO NOT TRY ME!

They say actions speak louder than words, your words so
flawlessly aligned, yet your act of love seemed like as if you
were walking on two right legs,

So out of rhythm, so out of meaning,

Soon after you learn that my tongue is a shade of armour
completed in colourful bruises,

You have mastered the art of rapid strategy to pull back all
the collateral tragedies you have so poorly caused,

It cost you losing me to learn that I am not a piece of bone
from a man's rib,

I am not a bonfire for your cold inanimate heart to warm
marshmallows,

I am not a flesh Scribbled in weaknesses waiting to be loved,

I am not a damsel dressed in distress afraid to stumble and
fall on my face first,
I am way beyond your black ice sculpture, beaming iridescent
dusts of dawn ,

So don't ask me to fly, after you have plucked my feathers to your likings,

Extending your age old begging to ride and die for your short comings,

Hiding devious insults under the walkway of our lawn covered in cobblestones,

A wordsmith irrationally abusing and abducting the flames in my light,

Surrounded by an ocean of your cackling jack O lanterns in the middle of the night,

Knees weak, fur worn out ,you thought?

Oh, I am mountains full of fight and rivers full of life , you see,

Drowned in the noises of harassers, you see,

The untameable outburst of rage , you see,

The clipped winged creature, a standing monument of greatness so moveless, you see,

So dare doubt my insanity,

When you blindly wade mindlessly in the clutch of your own
inhumanity.

10. WHAT SHAME ?

Words have a way of carrying secret bullets in them,

Ammunition echoes of "Since when did my body became an apology? ",

Comparing me to a "dismantled", "disfigured", "engineering gone wrong" handgun!

As if I had caused havoc on to the sight of your already sore eyes,

Becoming the filth under your shoes expecting me to curl up seeking for forgiveness,

As if I had run into a complex equation completed in wrong answers, leaving with no correct solutions,

As if I was a cavity full of useless emotions, fed with processed pollutions,

I am confused, how did My body become a prison to serve your perspectives?

Last I checked, I am still the gates to my body's needs,

Pouring light along my bones writing it's every deeds,

Falling and rising through the mistakes from which I have healed,

Walking into a doctor's office for asthma and getting prescribed "exercise"

When it hurts in this body to exist, demons suggesting to stop existing,

So believe me when I tell you I do not owe you a shroud of thinness or even the attempt of skinny-ness,

My heart is filled with passion and strength,

For that my blood strollers to length.

11. CHILD FROM POVERTY

Once upon a time she use to question the skies,

Hoping for a sign, hoping for answers ,hoping for solutions , seeking for validations,

She earned education as money by sweeping messes in mass spaces,

Cooking in stranger's homes,

Read through "hand me down books" with wrinkles and torn pages,

Resented gentrification yet admiring the refinement,

Attended school drenched in mud swimming through a sea of swine,

Risked every day to be a victim for an alligator's crime,

Vicious bites of neglect, violence , social deprivation, child rape and so much more she had to take,

She kept remembering that tomorrow is another day, where she had to do this all over again,

Yet her mother never warned her that she is an open feast for creatures that lurks in the night,

She never asked of her to stay away from the murky waters,

Never scared to find her children left behind the dark corners
of a trash can covered in blood, mangled and massacred ,

This little girl found beauty in her hustles,

Beauty in the burning city of her heart,

Found her place in the world outside of the kitchen by
purging her way through it all,

Liquidated the terrors and wiped it whole,

Though she lay in her bed of slumber, a still silk river,

She dreams of the ghosts that hunts her,

Forcing herself to grow into a blade hidden in a back pocket,

Hoarding the deaths of her supposedly murdered demons,

Marching in her empty halls painting great fortitude on to
her shadowy walls full of reasons.

12. BURNING JEALOUSY

These dimmed lights have you looking a little drowned in that blazing Victorian robe,

Let your pores feel the light won't you,

Have the flares on these alluringly calculated candles cast away your wall of fears,

Let those weighing fabric breathlessly slip off your silky shoulders,

At the business end of this dining table

you savour all the right words just to warm up the room,

Science once again teases me, condensation spreading everywhere ,

All those water droplets trailing down your ribs, I see the reflection of fire dancing,

Flickering every multi-coloured impatience in my bones,

The burning jealousy heaping through my blood,

For all the way the cutleries get to feel your fingertips, your lips,

The light that gets to touch your unveiled quirks,

The shadows that just sits in every detail of your nooks and
crannies,

I'll dance through these tremors if I have to, just let me enjoy
the view.

13. MEMORIES

How fond are we with our memories, every life begins in a sort of chaos, a destructively constructed product of a woman's sorrows and a man's egotism. Foul play, one might say.

In our own little ways, aren't we all addicted to the thought of freedom? Our bodies are constantly shackled to the cuffs wrinkled by our traumas, no cream or soap to make them disappear. Our trust, innocence, dependability, barriers being robbed by the misogynists left with no insurance to back them up. Similar to a wrecking ball, plundering every single bonding that holds everything together into tiny uneven rocks. To decide what shall be done of these crumbles of stones we stare at every single day, wondering how to mend all of them back together, to a time where pieces of sweet lights drizzle from a dark cloud , hovering through the atmosphere, defying gravity yet still so heavy, barring all that density. Our memories are our dark clouds, and the sky is full of them. Lilies wilted, would weep to everything my memories were and everything my memories will never be without me.

14. LETTER FROM MY SELF-DESTRUCTION

My dear dear lover,

Surrender to the pain won't you,

I promise you if you do I will show the stars,

You look so beautiful in pale blue skin, just look at you, so drained out,

Let me slither my lace all over your fragile chest and into your lungs,

Let my love for you sore through your bones,

Your heart is big they say, yet not strong enough I would say,

So let me hold it and lay it down,

I can take you to the sun where everything is so much mor brighter, my love!

Everything, I shall become of you as I love your most crude self,

Mutating through ever part of your cells like a composed orchestra,

Let our love grow, we can waste away together and let our harmony swell baby!

So stop trying to push me away, you really think you can just pop some pill or wrap me up in a book and kill me?

Fine, you take your time, I'll wait in the shadows of your scattered heart, quietly and calmly ,

Till you decide to let go of the shields you hold so firmly against me,

Convinced that I most probably must have given up on my foolish fantasies,

Grown weary through the wait and walked out on my destiny,

Then one day you would wake up and walk straight through the loop you built from ropes, that would clench on to your neck and hug it as you dangle on to the ceiling fan so beautifully,

That's when you will realize, I have come back for you and I alone am your only consistency,

So why fight me lover? Let us float away in radiance, like how I imagined us to be.

Yours everlasting love

Self-destruction.

15. OUR LOVE

You drew me into your beautiful words of oceanography,

Making memories that sit on the branches of a breath taking willow tree,

As I let myself drown out the sound of tragedy,

This uncontrollable need to escape has reached its peak,

Set sailing to the very core of freedom,

Taking my darkness under the tide bounding them to the decaying anchor,

How could my nights ever be too unkind,

When our love voyage began from sights of melting snow,

The aesthetic wilderness we lined up from clouds,

Infinite toxic wounds we carry through uncertainty,

So we let those question float into the atmosphere, maybe one day they can pop open into the words of our biography,

Maybe then we shall see the beauty of our symphony.

16. LOST SOUL

There is something in the air, it feels routined,

The morning scent of the sipping coffee, the freshly brewed aroma swirls around in the wind,

Watching the world take flight moving forward with all the consequences to follow,

Everyday seems to be the same fight haunted by those same fright,

Waiting through this youth for a solution when our ancestors wounded this world with oppression and confusion,

Outside this box sized bed there is something alluring in the music,

It has travelled from miles beaming rays of hope, looks like times are colliding,

Sounds like peeled off petals have been forced to wilt for generations,

A victim has always been the anchor of every lost ship, a balance to an uncontrollable drift,

These patterns of scared little sailors run in a predictable line,

Six hundred feet deep fears dressed in five hundred degree Celsius of anger,

What are your still hiding for?

There is nothing new you could show us! Nothing you have been through that someone else out there somewhere haven't been through,

Do not allow your demons to tell you, you are alone,

You have been left to be lost by another lost soul.

17. HER SILENT STRENGTH

Her heart pours heavier than a cloud of blood rain,

Spiralling traumas from the history hidden deep under the soils of her darkness,

Her songs of strength built layers of paint onto the Tuscan sun,

Her palms, as soft as cotton they maybe, her courage could slice storms into tiny slivers,

Do not test her ocean, you see, her tears swims in the dark Dead Sea,

The sky in her eyes have choked so many typhoons, she makes horror scream,

Her language holds a remix of her past and present,

The warm scent of spring and the pure white of winter,

Such vivid cinematography on repeat,

A nonstop machine thinking she could never be on her knees,

The world reminds you how you would break

Yet you still run no matter what it takes,

How long do you plan to bathe the planet in smiles of fake,

When the fights you fought were your butchered raw steak.

32

18. VANISHING IN MY PAST

This cave once knew me so well,

It's a shame the foundation never fit the name home,

Wall to wall constructions holding frames of barred windows,

Wasn't too sure if I was being protected or they were
protecting themselves,

This was the cage that chained me in,

With all the wounds and my broken shadows,

Neighbours with the longest nose

Spinning rumours clouding just outside my doors,

This place, meant for breathing meant for healing failed the
meaning of a sanctuary,

As much as my blood ran through the corners of this widely
spaced yet congested box,

The air in this habitation still reeks of the spots I left my past,

Feeling like the closed curtains never really lasted,

Struggling to float on the tears I lost,

That brassy fisted punches clogging my lungs,

The raging fire that burnt everything inside of me and left
ashes of resentment,

I always stayed hidden in the room where the water runs,
wading in the echoes of my furious grieving,

Getting up with everything left inside of me after every flog
of beating,

Though these floors have seen little sprinkles of laughter,

They sat on a dark loaf of bread covered in fungus waiting
like a ticking disaster,

I tried several times to fly away,

The thing with flying in closed eyes is,

You never know if your too close to the sun or too close to
the moon, either way you're still vanishing in empty space.

19. FATIGUING DISTRICT

My patience is running strait,

The nuances clutching on to my shades of horror,

They refuse to remain winced,

No matter how much I paint the sea full of roars,

Those tedious minds that trespasses through the gates I built in blood,

Amused by the abuse that follows to spark my fuse,

I find myself drained from preparing faces for such an aggravating phase,

Scuttling the chains of strength preserved in me,

Covered in a subdued cloak of isolation,

Detaching from all the goods of my own creations,

Drenched in all the fools approaching and seeking "stick for brain" conversations,

The amber sky can see the mad land I walk on,

The clouds have far beyond shrivelled to the fatiguing district,

Trying to goad my tolerance into a lunatic,

Swiftly I shall soon set my sails,

Eager paddling with no tracks to trail,

Soaring pages of the voyage I wrote,

Unbound to a master for I command my own boat.

20. SLOW STORMS

(Fibonacci form)

Slow

Nights

Of storms

Cannot stop

Me from running far

Beyond the hills of disarray,

So let death try and sneak its way under my door steps,

While I discretely two step sprint my way into the sweetest peak of my existence.